THE WAY WE LIVE
with the things
we love

STAFFORD CLIFF

THE WAY WE LIVE
with the things we love

WITH COLOR PHOTOGRAPHS BY

GILLES DE CHABANEIX

RIZZOLI
NEW YORK

Previous pages:
(*page 1*) A *Jugendstil* mosaic from a Viennese apothecary's shop depicts an angel holding aloft a golden bowl.

(*page 2*) A vase and a model boat are the prize posessions of two antique wooden mannequins, formerly dressed for traditional festivals in eastern Slovakia, now collectibles displayed in an open-air museum in Poprad.

Personal treasures displayed sparingly in this stylish, timeless interior *(right)* reflect the personality of their owners in a perfect balance of display and reserve. There is no clutter, and each object is given its due.

THE WAY WE LIVE
with the things we love

The grouping of contemporary elements in a illustrator's New York loft (*right*) develops the artist's workspace as a decorative theme. Pictures leaning against the wall suggest a gallery, while the collection of black and white bowls and vases, assembled in a composition reminiscent of a potter's drying shelves, forms the visual centrepiece of the room, drawing together the Bertoia chairs and eccentric cowhide upholstery.

(*page 6*) By bringing together objects from disparate cultures, rooms can be made to express both a selection process and individual eclectic tastes. Here hand-woven rugs, an Indian bed, and antique and contemporary pots create a harmonious composition in a modern space.

INTRODUCTION

The flea market (*opposite*) is the starting point for many collectors and interior designers. Here the hunt begins. Jumbled in confusion in this square in Brussels are objects that will come together in new compositions, in new homes. In other countries, car-boot sales, charity shops and designated days for putting unwanted furniture out on the street provide similar opportunities for collecting.

This book is not concerned with what to collect, or where to find it, but with how to display the things you find or buy to their best advantage, while keeping them protected and under control. Old shoes in the closet will look unremarkable, but a single brogue from the 1920s, spot-lit in a glass vitrine, will look amazing. Likewise, a collection of mismatched white plates will remain unnoticed in a stack in the kitchen, but mounted and hung in the living room against a white or pale grey wall, with their different embossed patterns catching the light, they will sparkle and glow.

Maybe you don't even think of yourself as a collector. You enjoy going to flea markets and antique shops, buying things that catch your eye or stir your imagination; you treasure family mementos and unexpected gifts from friends; you stroll along a beach picking up shells and pebbles. You bring these things home and integrate them with the books on your bookshelf, group them together on a coffee table or a side console, or hang them randomly on your walls. In doing this you are creating your own personal museum, bringing things together – be they found objects, inherited keepsakes or carefully sourced collectibles – to tell your own story in your home.

On the other hand, you may have spent a lifetime slowly building collections of things you love. Collecting begins when we are very young, and is driven by our instinct to accumulate. As young children we collect miniature soldiers, stuffed animals, dolls and model cars; older children graduate to paper items such as cigarette-card cricketers, pop-star portraits, autographs, postage stamps and comic books. Food manufacturers frequently produce collectibles and free gifts to encourage children to buy their products. There are also traditional collectibles that vary from culture to culture: tokens in English Christmas puddings, *faveurs* in French apple tarts. Later these treasured keepsakes become kitsch items for the next generation to discover all over again. Adults develop passions for fine art, antiques and luxury objects that fetch astronomical prices and drive entire industries (think of Fabergé eggs or Swarovski crystal figurines). A devotee may spend years searching for that one last piece to complete a set; an early bird at a flea market may bag an unrecognized treasure that resurfaces hours later in an expensive

The carefully composed chaos (*opposite*) of an antique shop offers kaleidoscopic possibilities. How many of these objects will end up living together?

antique shop, possibly in another country. This is the thrill of the hunt, the source of the professional collector's adrenalin rush. But the final triumph – and the final challenge – is to display your trophies in a decorative setting worthy of their value – be it intrinsic, aesthetic or emotional. Properly displayed, a collection of chocolate moulds delights the eye and kindles the imagination just as well as a collection of priceless paintings.

The images in this book are by the remarkable French photographer Gilles de Chabaneix, who, with his eagle eye for a good decorative idea or a telling personal detail, spent 40 years photographing domestic interiors all over the world. One of the results is a fascinating compilation of images that celebrates the ways in which we integrate our favourite collections of objects into our homes. How do you display 100 antique mixing bowls, for instance, or 200 butterflies, or 300 seashells? What do you do with a restored food-vendor's cart, a collection of vintage comic books or a pile of elephant bones? Or, more conventionally, how do you make the most out of a group of mismatched family photos and an enormous antique dresser that competes with the rest of your decor? With so many people around the world – many of them talented designers – collecting and displaying their personal treasures in their homes, there are hundreds of great ideas in these images to inspire you.

The collecting bug is responsible for an awful lot of clutter. Our attachment to the things we love can become so intensely personal that it becomes difficult to cull or organize them properly. This is particularly a problem with inherited items: the china piglets or military regalia that one's parents collected rarely fit with their children's decor or interests. Inheriting such a collection presents considerable decorative problems and anxieties for benefactors, and consequently provides a constant source of wares for collectors' fairs, yard sales, flea markets and online auction sites. Hoarding is another pitfall of collecting. Some people have collections that are so valuable that they keep them in a bank vault, or have so many things that they are stored in boxes under the bed. Better – as one collector once advised me – to decide where you want things to go, be it a certain shelf or wall or cupboard, and when the space is full, you stop.

Collecting is not only about seizing on one particular type of object and finding as many variations of it as possible. It is also about giving personality to the home in the same

The collection process comes to fruition in this Paris apartment (*opposite*), where nearly every item has been bourne triumphantly home from flea markets and antique shops across Europe. From mis-matched café tables, odd glass vases and lead finials salvaged from demolished buildings, a composition miraculously emerges.

way that you accessorize your wardrobe, using items that cannot be purchased in mainstream stores. Some people's entire homes are collections of things they love: pieces inherited from relatives and friends; restored chairs from junk shops or auction houses; tables and shelves made from recycled wood; fireplaces and doors from salvage yards; rewired lamps and light fittings – but nothing that came new from a shop. Sometimes a passion for a particular time period drives a collection: Victorian, Art Deco, the 1970s and 1980s. A collection can also be focused on a single country: African, Indian, the American Southwest, or a generic 'country cottage' style. A lifetime of accumulation can be melded into a seamless recreation of the past to fit the period of your house, matched to a single colour scheme, or assembled into an complete themed interior to suit your wildest fantasies. Alternatively, the whole decorative plan of a room can be arranged around one or two striking personal treasures.

In the following pages, you will be taken on a whirlwind tour of the possibilities of living with your possessions. For the sake of clarity, I have grouped Gilles's images according to the type of objects they depict: natural or machine-made; rare or everyday, religious, tribal or ethnic. But, as you will find in your own collections, most of the pictures contain objects belonging to more than one category. Whatever the nature of the 'things you love', there are not only infinite ways of framing, hanging or placing objects, but more importantly, ways of combining, juxtaposing, balancing, creating rhythm or impact; achieving wit and irony, contrast, scale and emotion. Space is also an important element, and one of the most difficult aspects to get right in a display. Surrounding an object with enough 'air' or negative space will add to the drama. This compilation provides an abundance of solutions to inspire you, and might even give you new ideas for things to collect.

Whether you have been accumulating and displaying your collections for generations, or are just beginning to decorate your home, this book will show you the tremendous creative adventure that lies ahead.

Stafford Cliff

CHAPTER 1

FLEA MARKET

The display and storage of objects
found by chance in street markets

Accessible to all and universally popular, the market
is the great melting pot of life. Flea markets teach us
more about other cultures and people's everyday
lives than do visits to any museum. Flea markets (or
boot-fairs, jumble sales and antique fairs, as they are
variously called) are held regularly in most countries
throughout the world and vary in size from small to
enormous. Treasures from flea markets generally fall
into two categories: things bought as part of the
considered decorative scheme of a home – ranging
from tables and lamps to doorknobs and brass taps –
and things bought on impulse, which can be
displayed alone or grouped as part of a collection.
The unpredictability and variety of the flea market
attracts the hunter–gatherer in everyone. Finding
something beautiful amidst the chaos of a flea
market brings a surge of pleasure that far outweighs
the item's actual value.

It is early morning and the excitement in the market is palpable.
Bargains are to be had, but treasures are easy to miss. Connoisseurs,
often more knowledgable than the dealers, examine the goods with
close scrutiny.

(*previous pages*) The furnishings of a home in the Cévennes are clearly a collection of 'finds' from a variety of flea markets and antique shops, but the casual informality of their arrangement gives them dignity and harmony. The placement of the Louis XVI *bergères* directs attention to the fireplace. The wall of pictures at left conveys a conventional old-fashioned elegance, but below the pictures, unexpectedly, a humble camp bed covered with pillows takes the place of a chaise-longue.

(*above*) This New York apartment has a theme, the art of the Navajo Indians, transported from its original context. The wooden object fixed to the wall above the chest is so-called 'tramp art', once commonplace remainder, now eminently collectable.

This Paris apartment does not insist on harmony in its decor. The clutter on the table recreates the market stall from which the objects displayed on it might once have come, and the furniture is arranged in a similarly casual manner.

(*left*) The world in a corner. The owner of this island home in Greece brings together a battered old boat, a classical head and an assortment of pots and vases in a striking three-dimensional composition.

(*opposite*) In a New York apartment the contents of the shelves are eclectic, with books and objects of all sorts grouped together, but the whole collection is disciplined by being strictly contained inside the wall unit. Turning some of the books to face outward adds another graphic element to the display. Flexible lighting on the shelves allows the owner to illuminate his ever-evolving collection to maximum effect.

Here, too – in a San Francisco apartment – the rigid boundaries of the cupboard give a definitive identity to the hundreds of beloved porcelain figurines squeezed together on the shelves with little thought for composition, apart from the smaller objects being placed in front.

In contrast, the flea-market finds displayed on shelves in this Sicilian house bear witness to a strong instinct for symmetry and the art of juxtaposition. The display is an exercise in abstract design, emphasizing the negative space between the shelves as much as their contents.

(*left*) The presentation of books can convey a drama of its own, although the books themselves (mainly lightweight vintage comics) might not conventionally be seen as objects of value. Displaying books behind glass doors has the added advantage of keeping them free of dust.

(*opposite*) Baskets become works of art (and why not?) if arranged with sufficient finesse and exhibited with an eye to composition. This French cupboard is a miniature gallery, not just a storage space.

(*left*) The living room of a house near Budapest is furnished like a shop – down to the antique apothecary's cabinet – with every item meticulously stored in its place.

(*opposite*) In a Naples apartment, various coloured shapes stand out against a white dresser. The arrangement is casual, the objects nothing special, yet they attract the eye and have been put together with a deliberate plan. A Philippe Starck chair in the foreground adds an explicit modernist touch.

Contrasts of colour can be used subtly without seeming contrived. This French interior neatly separates the colourful antique stuffed animals on the shelves from the prevailing neutral colour of the white-washed pine walls. The generous shelves leave ample space to display the owner's constantly enlarging collection.

(*left*) The mantelpiece provides an ideal opportunity for incorporating a variety of shapes into a single composition. These four fireplaces show the many possibilities for arranging groups of eccentric and unusually shaped objects on mantelpieces.

(*opposite*) Alternatively, the whole fireplace can function as a stage for showing off flea-market finds. This unusual corner-fireplace in a Scottish room incorporates Delft tiles, a model boat, a *papier-mâché* tray, and virtually anything else that might subsequently be added.

(*left*) Mixed collections of objects are especially effective arranged in front of framed pictures or a mirror on the mantelpiece, suggesting windows opening on to infinite other worlds.

(*opposite*) A mantelpiece display in a room in Milan creates a magical effect through repetition rather than variety, amassing an impressive collection of a single type of object – mirrored-glass candlesticks holding burning candles.

Another way of attracting the eye is to encourage it to focus at first not on the collection of objects, but on the furniture that supports them, be it a simple folding console table (*left*), a battered wooden chest (*right*) or a shelf crammed with books (*opposite left*).

(*above right*) Incorporating a few
continuously changing elements
keeps a display interesting. Plants
can be brought in from the garden,
pages of a book can be turned and
candles and fresh flowers replaced in
different arrangments.

(*opposite*) Desks are excellent platforms for displaying a diverse collection of objects in a vertical space. Each of these compositions tells a story that adds another dimension to the work actually done on the desks.

(*right*) Globes, pictures of lakes, scenic postcards, a model boat: this desk evokes the theme of journeys, real and imagined.

(*left*) A novel idea from Haiti: a wall of contrasting picture frames, each containing a mirror, adds sparkle and depth to a dimly-lit hallway.

(*opposite*) Old picture frames and framed pictures are displayed inside a salvaged casement window. The frame becomes the object framed – an exercise in conceptual ambiguity.

(*opposite*) The symbolic heritage of old specimen cases and hunting trophies – now carried home as trophies from flea markets and junk shops – makes them objects of fascination in otherwise tame interiors, where they evoke the thin line between life and death, predator and prey.

(*right*) The traditional display of wall-mounted animal heads as hunting trophies is given an ironic twist in the entrance hall of a San Francisco apartment, where a stuffed plush goose, a tin duck and a miniature replica deer's head greet the visitor returning from the hunt.

Two survivals from an age when every aristocrat's house was decorated by trophies of the chase: tusks, heads and a crocodile skin from African big-game hunting expeditions, probably from the 19th century, displayed in a stately home in Sicily (*left*) and more local quarry, including red deer and a mountain goat, in a house in Grenoble (*opposite*).

(*opposite*) A few whimsical objects can give an unexpected character to a room. Two antique pull-toy horses confront each other while a *papier-mâché* sheep's head and framed illustrations of exotic insects interrupt the stately calm of this otherwise conventional living room.

(*right*) It is always intriguing to find objects that are not in themselves bizarre but are placed in unusual settings. In this Paris apartment, the garden chairs have been moved indoors, and a leopard-skin stool drawn up beside them, for a meal of what appears to be live fish (actually sculptures) with a centrepiece of shells arranged in the shape of a human face. A Japanese-inspired painting completes the eccentric ensemble. These unexpected juxtapositions instantly engage the viewer in the story of the room.

(*opposite*) Six compositions, each creating a considered but unpretentious display by clustering groups of beloved objects – spectacles, coloured bottles, a box of dice, even a miniature castle – on side tables. In many cases a lamp is incorporated into the display.

(*right*) A vivid decorative effect can be created simply by encouraging the viewer's curiosity, as in this sideboard display in a house in Milan. The poseable figurines of a man and a woman are probably Iberian religious icons, but the tin architectural finials and flowered chandelier candelabrum offer no clues to the figures' identities.

(*overleaf*) A group of unrelated objects can also suggest a story opening *in media res*. Old documents, a ribbon, a Madonna, a jar of seashells and a trailing vine are arranged around a locked chest on the table in this French house as if recently abandoned in haste.

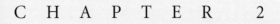

CHAPTER 2

TRIBAL

Decoration and detail from ethnic art around the world

The most potent of all the collectibles are the artefacts from tribal and traditional cultures throughout the world. Some of these objects are imbued with mystical or ritual significance for their makers; others are mundane household items; but for most collectors, the exotic design and timeless craftsmanship of 'tribal' artefacts gives them special decorative power. Masks look dramatic grouped together on a wall or supported on thin stands. Shields, headdresses, woodcarvings, pottery and small stools can be displayed alone or integrated with items from other periods or cultures. Though it may seem like a cliché, the plinth – even one only a few inches high – is still the best way to make an exotic item look extraordinary.

A row of ceramic bottles outside a pottery in Marrakesh. Viewed through new eyes in a different setting, these ordinary utilitarian objects become exotic treasures suggesting far-flung journeys.

(*left*) A row of masks and ancestral figures from Mali and Cameroon transforms a reading desk into a museum display.

(*opposite*) African masks and images of rice gods from the Philippines are juxtaposed with abstract sculpture and paintings in the Paris apartment of fashion designer Kenzo Takada. A single pebble on a small plinth is elevated to the status of a sculpture, while also suggestive of a votive offering.

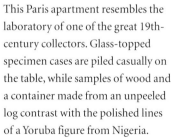

This Paris apartment resembles the laboratory of one of the great 19th-century collectors. Glass-topped specimen cases are piled casually on the table, while samples of wood and a container made from an unpeeled log contrast with the polished lines of a Yoruba figure from Nigeria.

In another Paris apartment, a more formal table-top assemblage suggests an altar, with offerings of fresh peonies and incense arranged at the feet of two Chinese funerary figures from the Han dynasty.

Common raw materials – in this case, honey-coloured wood – link an African carving of a woman with the framed Western engravings on the landing, a table displaying a selection of Chinese vases, and the angular modern stairs she seems to have just descended.

A reproduction of one of the famous Qin dynasty terracotta warriors stands guard beside the doorway of a Los Angeles house. The plain walls and stark clay tones of the concrete floor banish any hint of kitsch from the mass-reproduced figure.

(*previous page*) Kuba appliqué cloth, an African carved stool and a Japanese kimono rack add bold dark elements that draw the eye in a monochromatic white living room in Mallorca. The three blade-like objects in the centre of the room are a traditional type of currency used in Zaire.

(*above*) Ethnic art can bring an element of formality to contemporary spaces, as in this living room in Monte Carlo. The Senufo and Bambara animal carvings mounted on unadorned plinths suggest museum displays, in contrast to informal elements such as the folding deck chairs, bamboo table and tile floors. The dark wood of the carvings transforms the smoke-staining around the fireplace into a central decorative feature.

Alternatively, tribal elements can be introduced to soften the formality of an interior. The earth tones of Malian mud-resist cloth and a carved wooden masquerade head from Nigeria contrast with the elaborate blue window grille, transforming the corner of the room into an inviting space for relaxing.

The clean, bold patterns of Kuba appliqué cloth from Zaire, stretched and framed like paintings, fit the square angles and metal tones of a minimalist, ultra-modern interior in Sicily as if they were abstract artworks painted to order.

Shields, hides, pots, carvings and lengths of cloth are stacked against the walls of a living room in a careful composition designed to suggests the haphazard jumble of a merchant's stall or royal treasure house filled with tribute.

In the living room of a home converted from a former brick factory in New Jersey, a battered Senufo bed from Mali makes a dramatic statement, interacting with the dark colour and rounded contours of a conventional Western leather-covered armchair.

The dark walls bring out the rich earth and ochre colours of the Kuba appliqué cloth, here used as the canopy for a bed in which one can imagine sleeping beneath the African stars. An Ethiopian basket in the foreground adds a splash of colour among the black and white objects displayed on a plain black table.

Staircases, landings and passages are the transitional spaces of apartments and houses. Their comparatively awkward shapes often provide a great challenge for the interior decorator and designer. Staircases, in particular, can provide additional display areas, both for paintings and for three-dimensional works of art, especially those with elongated forms, such as this Malagan carving *(above)* from Melanesia displayed in the corner of a Parisian apartment.

(above) Elongated totem-pole-like carvings also work well along the edge of a window, contrasting with the squat forms of the bathtub and chairs in this bathroom in Corsica.

(opposite) A careful assemblage involving a carved wooden granary door from Mali, an Ethiopian stool, and a ladle made from a coconut shell atop a set of contemporary bowls evokes mysterious and intensely feminine themes.

A staircase within a staircase: a tree trunk that once served as a temporary entrance ladder for a Dogon house in Mali becomes the focal point of the staircase in a Paris home, transformed into an abstract carving that draws the eye upward as it seems to reach toward the light.

In the Chilean rainforest is the estate of an American billionaire who is also a conservationist on a grand scale. All the living and utility buildings on the estate are built of local woods and designed to be eco-friendly – a fitting setting for the owner's extensive collection of ethnic art.

A living tree growing through a Tunisian house becomes the focal point of an all-white room, while on the wall behind it an elaborately painted traditional wooden cabinet explodes with colour and pattern.

Utilitarian items from different cultures come together in this Argenteuil loft conversion. The stark lines of an East African chair made from two slabs of wood echo the shape of the original factory stove, while a collection of Western and African archery equipment adorns the 'primitive' unfinished cinder block walls.

Traditional African drums are paired with contemporary paintings in a rustic Provençal home.

In a Paris apartment, a collection of grotesque masks and the stern features of a Senufo figure meet the gaze of anyone who pauses to admire his or her reflection in the mirror over the corner fireplace.

(*above*) A travel story unfolds on the mantelpiece of a French home. A globe, an ostrich egg and a vase of exotic orchids flank an antique African hairdresser's sign, whose absence of lettering encourages the viewer to interpret each object symbolically.

(*right*) Antique African hairdressers' signs, usually hand-painted on tin and depicting a range of available hairstyles, are now sought-after one-of-a-kind collectible items in the West.

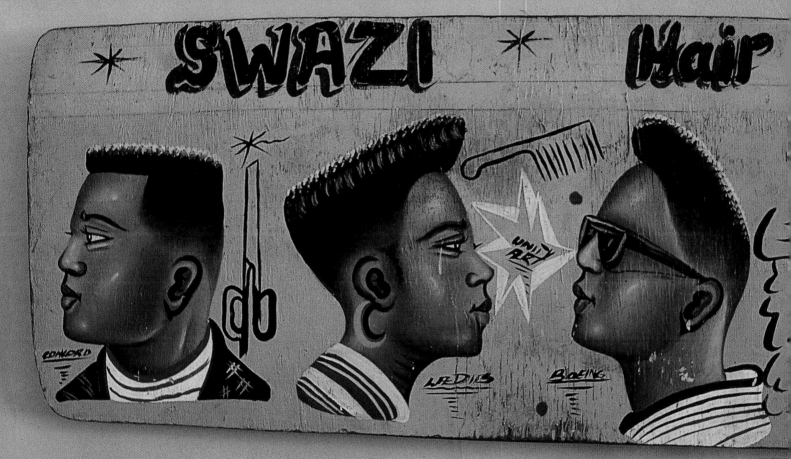

(*opposite*) A traditional Balinese woven bag suggests a modern graphic design when displayed flat against pale angular bamboo.

(*right*) Ethnic artefacts become contemporary decorations in this Mexican house. A woven straw basket full of eggs rests on a traditional axe-dressed work counter, which has been mounted on modern brushed-aluminium trestles whose shape echoes the pueblo-style ladder leaning in the corner.

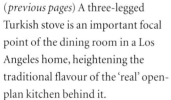

(*previous pages*) A three-legged Turkish stove is an important focal point of the dining room in a Los Angeles home, heightening the traditional flavour of the 'real' open-plan kitchen behind it.

(*above*) Glass-fronted cabinets offer a simple but effective way to display ethnic art, here enclosing the dark woods of East African carvings inside simple white-painted 'frames'.

A similar assemblage in a London home uses the contrast of brown and white colours to connect the antique English bottles inside the glass-fronted cabinet with the Tanzanian water container hanging from the knob like a *trompe l'œil* extending into the frame of a painting.

Framing is an effective way to isolate groups of ethnic artefacts in an interior for a more structured look. Here, African-inspired sponge painting frames a selection of earthenware pots on the mantelpiece of a Paris home.

In a San Francisco bedroom, a framed reproduction of a Georgia O'Keefe painting is surrounded by Mexican and Native American objects from the area of the Southwest that inspired her work. A plain wooden cross grounds the composition, echoing the rough timber of the walls. Unfinished timber framing creates a conceptual separation between the assemblage on the dresser and the contrasting collection of baskets and Arts & Crafts-era ceramics displayed on the shelf above it.

TRIBAL

In the dining room of a Paris house belonging to a French fashion forecaster, the thick, strong contours of a group of Senufo stools from Côte d'Ivoire contrast with the airy insubstantiality of the gauze-draped industrial table, while hinting at the heavy wooden structure beneath the tablecloth.

The plain, dramatic shapes of Senufo stools make them an ideal component in a wide range of modern interiors. In this casual, unfussy house in Île de Ré, the stool amplifies the natural resonances of the wooden floor, beige walls and undyed upholstery fabric.

(*above*) A Senufo stool is equally at home in the sleek minimalist bathroom of a Los Angeles house. Its presence in the bathroom is particularly appropriate, as Senufo stools are also used as washstands in their native Mali and Côte d'Ivoire.

(*opposite*) A Nupe stool from northern Nigeria and a table from Cameroon bring an air of exotic luxury to the library of a Paris apartment. Despite their unusual shapes, these small pieces of African carved furniture can be incorporated successfully into any room in the home.

TRIBAL

This traditional Provençal house near the village of Les Baux-de-Provence holds a multitude of diverse and exotic artefacts, yet all are personally valued by the owners and have been marshalled here to form a harmonious and balanced display. An enormous Baule Goli mask above the fireplace acts as a focal point, while other objects gathered during travels – including a stool from Cameroon in the foreground, carved with a spider motif – decorate the corners of the large, well-proportioned room.

A collection of Hopi pottery and kachina dolls from the American Southwest displayed in a Paris apartment. Groups of artefacts collected from a single culture can create a coherent decorative scheme that emphasizes the variations within – rather than between – cultures. Both aesthetic tensions are at play in this interior, with groups of Hopi objects alternating with groups of modern Western artworks.

Rustic woods draw together the Southwestern American elements in the corner of a San Francisco home: cactuses, Navajo saddle blankets, a weather-beaten tin sign and a mission-style armchair.

TRIBAL

Ethnic jewelry can adorn the home
as well as the body. Shell necklaces,
breast-plates and body jewelry from
New Guinea and the Solomon
Islands are displayed on stands in
front of a row of 19th-century
photographs of Native Americans.
Bowls of dried and fresh flowers
complete the three-tier assemblage
in this Paris apartment.

CHAPTER 3

ART HOUSE

The domestic display of prints, photographs, paintings and sculpture

Hanging a few pictures on the wall should be a simple decorative task, but often isn't. If the frames, styles and subjects are all different, it can be difficult to create a coherent display from a collection of beloved artworks. A good display of art considers not only the size and the colour of the works, but also the types of frames, and the negative spaces between them. Another solution is to line up a row of framed pictures on a single long narrow shelf, or – if the pictures are large enough – simply to lean them against the wall. Sculptures can be placed on unconventional plinths such as stairs or windowsills, and fine-art glass and ceramics also benefit from a 'sculptural' decorative treatment. Whichever method is used, the effect is dramatic when art is displayed well.

Art dealers, decorators and amateur collectors choose from among thousands of artworks at the London Art Fair. Many of these works will at some point be displayed in a home. Although a certain amount of taste and skill is required, the decorative possibilities are endless.

ART HOUSE

An extreme expression of the 'Art House' theme: this home in Paris could at first be mistaken for a gallery. Everything, even the chairs, look like works of art. Glass display cases, high ceilings and generous floor space magnify the gallery-like atmosphere.

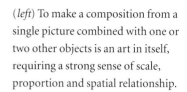

(*left*) To make a composition from a single picture combined with one or two other objects is an art in itself, requiring a strong sense of scale, proportion and spatial relationship.

(*opposite*) A strong black and white picture in a heavy dark frame imposes a sense of order on the room, emphasizing the square, classical lines of the mantelpiece. A row of seashells, whose naturalistic curves are repeated in the abstract paint-work on the fireplace, softens the severity of the arrangement and bridges the conceptual space between the two squares, while keeping a low profile along the top of the mantelpiece.

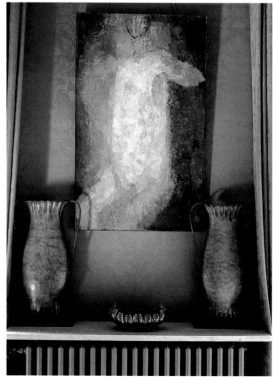

Judging from the pictures, bedside lamp and ornaments in this Paris bedroom, the owner's tastes run decisively to the baroque. The bed, however, reflects a modernist sense of austerity. These contrasting – yet complementary – themes are communicated dramatically by the picture frames. On one side of the room the frames are heavy, dark and unadorned; on the other, a light gilded wood. Because the variously sized pictures are arranged along a single base-line, the effect is oddly harmonious: a subtle but effective technique for combining different decorative tastes in a single room.

Parisian restraint: black and white photographs in plain wooden frames hang in a rigidly symmetrical arrangement flanking the centreline of a bed in neutral colours. This arrangement can be used to create an illusion of space and openness around a narrow bed, or in a small room such as a guest bedroom.

(*opposite*) In a home in the south of France, the owner has used a simple but dramatic method of displaying framed artwork. Pictures lean against the walls as if in an art dealer's warehouse, lit by a single workman's utility light, which can be moved from picture to picture.

(*right*) This Paris apartment also cultivates the ambience of an art gallery, with sculptures mounted on plinths and pictures leaning against the wall. This corner composition plays with perceptions of size, creating an intriguing dissonance between the large picture of the man on the floor and the smaller sculpture of the elephant, which is mounted on a high plinth and confronted by a tiny human figure at its feet.

(*left*) A group of pictures by a single artist makes a bold statement in a muted palette. The close relationship between the paintings – and the variety among them – is also communicated by the frames, which are all made from the same dark wood, but of different thicknesses.

(*opposite*) The decorative scheme of this house in the Bragança Palace in Goa reflects the mixed Indo-Portuguese origin of the city itself. The 19th-century portraits on glass are European in idiom, but were produced in India. They have been carefully arranged so that the figures appear to look at each other. Three plates delicately fill the negative spaces between the pictures.

Dense groupings of small pictures create elegant, intricate displays in two very different interiors. The colour of the wall is particularly important in this type of arrangement, functioning as the matrix in which the pictures are embedded like small gems. An eggshell-blue wall (*left*) makes a collection of oils recede into the background for a subtle effect that emphasizes the brightness of the gilt frames, while a group of dark, muted artworks springs to life on a cream-coloured wall (*right*).

Pictures of uniform colour and theme create a dramatic effect when arranged closely together, particularly in a room dominated by a single, strong colour, as with the pen-and-ink drawings displayed against vivid ultramarine walls of this Paris apartment.

Alternatively, groups of matched pictures can be displayed against a similarly coloured background for an arresting monochromatic effect. Hung with very little space between them, these 19th-century engravings of moths in a Paris living room read as a single large work at first glance.

Another striking display using 'artworks' of uniform subject, size and colour. Framed entomological collections of butterflies and moths this dining room in Corsica recall the orderly containment of collections in a natural history museum. The lightness of the winged specimens draws out the airy quality of the room and introduces a subtle antique flavour into the decorative scheme as a whole. The collection of rare moths and butterflies was once a favoured gentleman's pastime but is now considered ecologically irresponsible. This display uses antique and ethically-sourced specimens.

(*opposite*) A varied but coherent and sophisticated display of black and white photographs in the bedroom of a Belgian apartment. Each framed work is of a different shape and size, but the collection – a mixture of personal photographs and art prints – has been assembled as a carefully composed geometric puzzle that fills an entire wall.

(*right*) A simlar decorative effect appears on the wall of a Paris home. Black and white drawings and engravings in different styles, shapes and sizes are fitted together as if on the page of a scrapbook, complementing the black and white furniture. An abstract painting enlivens the assemblage with a single splash of colour.

(*left*)A repeated theme can be used to lead the eye from one interior space to another. In a Paris home a consistent colour scheme and a collection of paintings featuring young women unite the two rooms into a single conceptual and decorative composition.

(*opposite*) In another Paris home, a single painting beside a door unites the two spaces when seen from this vantage point, incorporating the striking colours used in each room.

There is an entirely seductive quality about the relative informality of this sitting-room in a house in the hot region of south-west France. The collection of paintings – all portraits of women, incorporating vibrant red and yellow hues, which are echoed by the rugs and furniture coverings – is arranged around the central mantelpiece and mirror.

(*above*) In a holiday home on the Île de Ré, the arrangement of books, paintings and nautical models around the fireplace is carefully ordered, turning the whole wall into an area devoted to the owner's personal interests.

(*overleaf*) Pictures, sculptures and books in a single assemblage organized around African and colonial themes. The success of the composition depends on the fragile balance of the sizes and shapes of the objects and the spaces between them.

A striking background colour can unify large collections of small, random objects on a wall. Dozens of pictures and decorations in a child's room are arranged towards the ceiling on a powerful blue background, an approach that also prevents small children from knocking objects off the walls.

A collection of unframed family photographs arranged on shelves against a bright yellow wall. This is an easy and unpretentious method for displaying personal pictures, which can be moved around on the shelves without the need for replacing frames and moving hooks.

The very small black and white pictures arranged at random on the wall of a house in Bolinas, California, work on two levels. From a distance, the collection resembles an abstract relief sculpture. Up close, the individual photographs tell their own stories.

A rigidly horizontal arrangement of small framed pictures on a shelf creates a similar abstract sculptural effect, but is easier to achieve than the arrangement at left as it does not require picture hooks. Viewed up close, the lives of the room's inhabitants unfold on the horizontal plane like storyboard illustrations.

Family pictures displayed like a public scrapbook. The picture frames – made from cardboard and wood scavenged from fruit crates – set the tone of unfussy minimalism that dominates this city loft, and visually unify the family and friends shown in the pictures.

Family photographs in a Palermo home are clustered together like a collection of religious icons, interspersed with sketches and art photographs. Family members living and dead, real and imagined, form a great crowd in this powerful but unassuming display.

These three rooms represent the ultimate in picture-dominated interiors. An extraordinary collection of antique postcards, all depicting famous rocks, pushes the decorative device of grouping small pictures on a single theme to its inevitable – and surprisingly successful – conclusion (*opposite*), as does the collection of personal photographs displayed throughout a Paris apartment (*right*). In another apartment, a riot of pictures and handwritten letters, all hung deliberately askew, covers every wall surface. One could spend hours examining each piece (*below right*).

(*left*) These four interiors all demonstrate the infinite decorative potential of art pottery. Whether arranged alone or in groups, the shape, colour and texture of fine ceramics give them the aesthetic power of abstract sculpture.

(*opposite*) A group of ceramic objects in the corner of a Los Angeles house provides a particularly fine example of this sculptural effect: three pots placed on the floor, similar in colour but graded in size, form a room-sized installation with a bare branch and a single bowl set seductively in the next room.

(*overleaf*) There could hardly be a greater contrast than that between this carefully restrained monochrome composition of dark and clear vases in simple, modern shapes (*left*) and the riotous display of whimsical, candy-coloured Venetian glass, even though both are archetypal 20th-century styles that bring sparkle and reflection to any interior.

The home offers a far more flexible and varied display space than a gallery. In a home decor, mass-produced and folk artworks can be displayed alongside fine-art objects without any sense of disjuncture. A group of carved water-bird decoys adds a three-dimensional element to a row of framed fine-art paintings in a house in Normandy.

An unpretentious mass-produced carving of an elephant displayed on the sill of an open window lends a quiet dignity to the room.

(*above left and right*) The special decorative quality of sculpture is its three-dimensionality, which can be emphasized by displaying sculptural works where they will catch the light during the day and at night, perhaps from a flickering candle placed nearby. Both of these nudes benefit from being displayed near windows.

Two-dimensional objects and artworks – such as the pictures reflected in the mirror (*above left*) or the portrait of a man seen through the glass door (*above right*) can be arranged to interact with the sculptural elements in the room.

(*left*) Artist's stands bring the flavour of a sculptor's studio – rather than an art gallery, where sculpture is typically exhibited on plinths – to a collection displayed in the home.

(*opposite*) Sculptural works in radically different styles from two different periods – classical Greek and abstract modern French – are displayed on the same stand, projecting an aura of confidence and showcasing the owner's wide-ranging taste in art. The black and white colour theme unifies the diverse collection, even as it emphasizes the contrasts between the individual works.

CHAPTER 4

ANTIQUES

The best use of your most treasured possessions

Antiques are among the most unique collectibles, and generally the most expensive. When not inherited from family members, antiques are usually acquired in dedicated shops, auction houses or specialist fairs. The legal definition of an antique is an object that is at least 50 years old, but most are considerably older and often come with a specific provenance. The antique items in this chapter are frequently assembled to form entire rooms – even entire homes – decorated in the style of a particular period. Sometimes these collections are maintained within a family over several generations, constantly enlarged with the help of dealers, decorators and frequent trips to antique shops. Other collections are assembled by a single owner with a special passion for the style of a particular time period, such as Victoriana or 1960s pop-kitsch. The most inspiring rooms feel ageless, even as they invite the visitor to step back in time.

This is not the home of a lover of antiques, but almost a parody of one: reproductions of classical statuary in the prop-room of an Italian film company in Cinecittà, Rome.

(*above*) An antique globe, classical statuary and columns in the library of a home in Granada, Spain, are reminders of an age when European decorative taste prized the display of expensive antiques. With its curio cabinets, tiled floor and collection of Asian artefacts, this room could be mistaken for one of the great libraries of the Enlightenment.

(*opposite*) A classical seated figure, old manuscripts, an antique globe and an architectural model of a Gothic church seem perfectly at home alongside modern artworks in this country house in Pedraza, Spain.

This Paris study would seem bookish
and homely were it not for the
fantastic chandelier and the Art
Nouveau caryatids each side of the
window. These are plaster versions
of relief carvings that once adorned
a 19th-century building, inherited
from the owner's uncle.

A headless classical statue placed in a niche lends gravitas to a room in Hamammet, Tunisia. Beside the niche hangs a picture of a legless Mayan temple sculpture depicting the Young Maize god – another damaged monument of another fallen empire – which introduces multiple layers of conceptual contrast.

Classical statuary *in situ* at the Villa Medici in Rome: a classic, stately display of antiques, itself well over 400 years old.

A large collection of related pieces of
antique furniture in a high-ceilinged
room conveys the impression – real
or manufactured – of the seat of one
of the great, ancient families.

A room in the Closenberg Hotel,
Sri Lanka, includes antique furniture
arranged in a European manner
to give the impression of well-
established family ownership, but
the pieces here have been executed by
Sri Lankan craftsmen in a local style.

Portraits displayed on top of richly ornate chests create a distinctively Asian antique arrangement, reminiscent of Buddhist altars, which can be interpreted in a Western setting using classical busts or antique masks. A portrait page from an antique illuminated manuscript is flanked by candles on a carved chest in a home in Bali (*left*), and a similar arrangement in a museum–home in Bangkok incorporates an ancient stone head displayed atop a stunning gold-lacquered antique cabinet (*opposite*).

A complete antique interior makes a powerful and luxurious decorative statement. This magnificent room in the Casa Manila museum in the Philippines is completely decorated with 19th-century furniture (locally crafted in European-inspired styles) and ancient Chinese porcelain, conveying the timelessness and solidity of a long-established family dynasty.

The Bragança Palace in Goa follows a similar convention, in a sitting room entirely outfitted in antique rosewood furniture carved in a sumptuous 19th-century local style. In contrast to the immaculately preserved interior shown opposite, the peeling, elaborately painted walls and faded sepia photographs give the haunting impression that time has not stood still in this room, drawing attention to the extreme climate and the passing of the years outside its four walls.

(*left*) One exquisite piece of antique furniture is often enough to bring distinction to a room. Large free-standing cabinets, such as this brightly painted cupboard-desk in a Swedish home, offer useful storage as well as an antique decorative focus. Large ornate cabinets and wardrobes are easy to find in antiques shops, being much more frequently discarded by their original owners than smaller, plainer items of furniture.

(*opposite*) In the Villa Medici elaborately painted doors dominate an otherwise plain and sombre room. The fantastic wreaths and cherubs seem to beckon the visitor into an adjoining chamber of secrets.

(*overleaf*) Judging from the gilt-framed pictures and mirrors waiting to be hung on bare walls, one would guess that a wealthy family was still in the process of moving in to this high-ceilinged Provençal house. In fact, the half-finished look is deliberate and has been carefully constructed by the owners. This casual, minimalist display of expensive antiques offers an alternative to the conventional lush and often stuffy interiors of old stately homes.

Antique Spanish-style family portraits open like windows to the past in a house in Manila, bringing human faces to reinforce the 19th-century decorative theme of the rooms.

(*opposite*) A display of family portraits unfolds like a timeline in the Chigi Palace in Rome, reinforcing the impression of aristocratic continuity. The small icon-like portraits, begun when the foundations of the family were laid in the 17th century, are continued in the same style with identical frames into the 19th century, covering the walls of an entire room.

Family portraits spanning many generations are displayed beside a collection of antique glassware in the casual, cluttered dining room of a house near Budapest. The enormous collection of portraits crammed into a small space, in a fan-like arrangement reminiscent of a family tree, suggests the home of an eccentric survivor of a waning aristocratic dynasty.

The clutter of a single type of antiques makes a striking decorative statement in this Brussels apartment. Every inch of wall space is covered in corner sections of old picture frames and plaster wall mouldings, creating a surprising modern-looking abstract geometric effect.

ANTIQUES

The antiques in this Rangoon interior are displayed in a more sedate and uncluttered arrangement. The furniture consists of matched pieces in a modern Chinese-inspired design, whose simple lines and dark woods complement rather than compete with the more ornate antiques. A relatively small number of large decorative antique objects are distributed throughout the room with generous amounts of space between them.

Standing clocks are another distinctive antique frequently handed down through the generations, with vast numbers of unwanted examples consequently available in antique shops. They can be used to striking effect in tall, narrow spaces beside doors, or in crowded rooms such as kitchens. Depending on the clock, the decorative effect can be either stately – as in this pale-blue and gold English-inspired example (*left*) or cheerful and homely, as with this squat and gaily painted 19th-century Swedish clock (*opposite*).

Antique shelving brings a patina of age to the items displayed on it, and can serve as the decorative focus of a room in its own right. A monumental set of mahogany shelves with elaborately turned spiral posts is the first item to catch the eye in this eclectic living room, where a vast array of showy and deliberately contrasting antiques vie for attention.

The distinguished air of this
library–study in a Provençal house
does not come from the casually
arranged books and mixed furniture,
but from the shape of the room and
the original 18th-century panelling
and shelving that have been carefully
conserved by the present owner.

(*opposite*) Chinese script has always been cherished for its beauty, and features prominently in this tableau of Chinese antiques clustered around a battered traditional gaming table.

(*above*) A collection of graceful antique Japanese ceramics displayed behind sliding doors in a traditional wooden curio cabinet. A shared simplicity of form bridges the gap between the Asian antiques and the 20th-century Western tubular-steel chairs in the foreground.

(*above*) A successful pairing of traditional and contemporary Asian elements: antique Chinese vases arranged below modern artworks incorporating Chinese script.

(*overleaf*) Valuable antiques need not always be displayed solemnly. The antiques in these two Paris homes have been arranged to create amusing dialogues between objects.

(*pages 156–57*) In contrast to the lighthearted displays of antiques in the two Parisian houses, is this stiffly formal but spectacular room of a house in New York City (devoted entirely to antiques of the European Gothic Revival period from between 1840 and 1850), which still retains a personal flavour that keeps it from being mistaken for a museum.

C H A P T E R 5

RELIGIOUS

The decorative iconography of votive
images and artefacts

One need not be religious to collect and display
religious artefacts. Fans of these types of objects
appreciate them for their rich imagery and
materials, their honest and direct emotional appeal
and their distinctive regional craftsmanship.
Religious objects vary enormously in size, ranging
from tiny metal ex-votos and *milagros* to scale
models of churches and carved stone deities. Most
will look best standing together in groups or
hanging from walls or ceiling beams in related
clusters. Some small figures come with their own
plinths or shelves; larger items, such as life-sized
Buddhas or images of saints, look better placed
slightly above eye level, which is often how their
makers intended them to be viewed.

Religious objects in a church in Atacama, Southern Chile, need no
aesthetic rules to guide their arrangement – their power here is not
dependent on the eye. Displaying religious objects in a non-
devotional setting, however, presents a considerable decorative
challenge, requiring a sensitive and nuanced approach to preserve
their special beauty and dignity.

(*left*) A perishable and lighthearted but still striking religious artefact: a model church carved out of root vegetables, intended as a thanksgiving offering at an annual harvest festival.

(*opposite*) A more permanent model church in tin, possibly an antique tourist souvenir, displayed as part of a secular home decor on a hallway table, where passing breezes might make the miniature bells ring in the towers and the delicate angels spin around the spires.

(*opposite*) A quaint model church retains its calm religious aura amid the soft pastels of a house on the Île de Ré.

(*right*) This intriguing, unsettling 'shrine' assemblage in a New York house has been built around a wooden niche that once held a saint's image in a church interior. Preserved insects, images of snakes and lizards, and a strange reptilian standing figure, hands clasped as if in prayer, invite the viewer to contemplate a different set of mysteries.

(*above and opposite*) The house of a
singer in Budapest resembles the
premises of an antique dealer.
Beautiful and intriguing religious
objects are simply left where they can
find a place amid the secular objects:
pottery, medicine bottles, a butter-
mould, antique glass, needlework
cushions and naïve secular paintings.
In this chaotic display, images of
saints and an Agony in the Garden
are presented as part of the rich
hubbub and variety of life.

In a Paris home, a pilgrim's souvenir Madonna and Child in rusted stamped tin is a pretty decorative item that adds colour and texture to the plaster scrollwork behind it.

(*right*) An elaborate antique devotional image of the Coronation of the Virgin Mary is displayed not only for its themes of redemption and resurrection (echoed by the secular abstract paintings leaning against it) but also for the rich texture of its battered frame, which resonates closely with the ceramic vase and faded wooden display cabinet.

(*overleaf*) Devotional paintings still hang in the library of a former seminary, now a guest house and community centre, at San Cristóbal de Las Casas in the Chiapas region of Mexico. Retaining a few devotional elements in the decor of a religious building that has been converted to secular use acknowledges the history of the space.

In a home in Budapest, religious and secular keepsakes and decorations are displayed together on a crowded ledge, loosely organized by size and materials.

Some of the most successful decorative displays of religious artefacts deliberately elude dogmatic interpretation. A corona of saints, elegantly displayed on wire brackets, forms an arch over a painted cabinet in Milan, beckoning the eye to contemplate the brightly coloured shrine. The shrine is unexpectedly empty, inviting the viewer to imagine who or what might fill it.

RELIGIOUS

Like an altar for secret devotions, a two-tier display in the attic of a Milanese house includes worn religious figurines stripped of their identifying symbols (including an image of St Isidore, the patron saint of farmers, watching over a team of oxen drawing a plough) together with a collection of candlesticks, a battered tin shrine and a weathervane possibly salvaged from a church. The arrangement implies an altar dedicated to a group of saints, or to personifications of crafts and occupations of the past, but carefully avoids identifying the figures, inviting visitors to construct their own parables from the scene.

Single images of the Buddha bring an air of transcendental calm to any space in the home. A Buddha watching over the bathroom of a house in Bangkok (*above*) implies the cleansing of the spirit along with the body, turning an ordinary bathtub into a sacred pool

(*opposite*) Religious images are especially evocative in the transitional spaces of a home. A worn gilded Buddha sitting atop a pedestal cabinet in a Paris apartment invites passers-by to pause briefly for contemplation. The figure has been placed between two windows, which makes it appear as if an aura of light radiates from its gilt patina.

Pairing a religious sculpture with an object from nature creates a simple, beautiful composition. A damaged wooden Buddha, with a round, smooth pebble replacing the right hand, is lit dramatically by the slanting light of the sun.

Another unusual Buddha is covered in gold leaf and carries a simple offering of frangipani blossoms around his neck. As with the figures in the two preceding images, this Buddha has been placed deliberately in the light from a window, making the worn gold-leaf skin seem to glow from within.

(*left*) A tin image of Kuan Yin, the Chinese goddess of mercy, presides over the treasures on an artist's desk: a Creole doll, cigarette lighters, shells, matchboxes and a lamp made from recycled beer cans.

(*opposite*) A *tokonoma* is a traditional Japanese alcove display that harks back to the great houses of the old samurai families. These slightly raised alcoves, usually opening in to a drawing room or tea-ceremony room, are typically decorated with Chinese luxury items, such as the scroll, plate and vase displayed on the wall in this example, with the addition of a collection of ornate Chinese ink boxes scattered at the Buddha's feet. Other *tokonoma* centre on a vase, which holds flowers that represent the season of the year. The jutting pillar made from the unfinished trunk of a cedar tree is also a traditional feature.

(*left*) A selection of decorative compositions in bedrooms featuring religious imagery, ranging from traditional rosary beads (*top right*) or an embroidered cross (*top left*) to a spectacular collection of candlesticks and golden icons (*bottom left*) or the plain, almost abstract cross in a London home (*bottom right*).

(*opposite*) A strange, fantastic crowd of naïve Christian folk images – including a monumental figure from a crucifix and a Madonna in a gold dress receiving the Annunciation from an absent angel – covers every inch of a bedroom dresser, whose cracked mirror suggests an otherworldly dreamscape. A winged Indonesian tiger, a plastic dinosaur and a crystal camel complete the surreal fairy-tale assemblage.

(*opposite*) In the hallway of a Los Angeles home, the seated Buddha in his niche strikes a single dramatic note that requires no elaboration in the minimalist decor and monochromatic colour scheme.

(*right*) An image of the Hindu god Shiva stands in a simple niche over the swimming pool in a Paris apartment, flanked by bamboo seen through the picture windows. Niches are natural places to display religious images in the home – they echo the decor of temples and churches, and visually acknowledge the other-worldly aspect that gives religious artefacts their decorative power.

Sacred Buddhist images displayed in a niche in a traditional Japanese house. Religious imagery in its proper setting inspires its decorative use in the home. There is a clear conceptual connection between this traditional Buddhist shrine and its secular interpretations in the homes on the two preceding pages.

CHAPTER 6

RUSTIC

The charm of found objects from nature

Nature is one of the most readily available decorative resources, and the most plentiful. A large leaf, picked up in a rainforest and pressed into the bottom of a suitcase, can look like a piece of art when framed and hung on the wall at home. Likewise – providing restrictions don't prevent importing them – seed pods can be displayed like exotic treasures or abstract sculptures. Nearer to home, things found on beaches or riverbanks – pebbles, seashells, ammonites and driftwood – make unusual and personal treasures when mounted on plinths or grouped together on a shelf or a desk. Natural found objects look wonderful in any home decor, cost nothing, and bring the beauty of the outdoors inside, evoking the smell of the woods and the crash of waves in the wild places where they were collected.

The island of Bora Bora in the Pacific is a natural setting for sophisticated rusticity. A cabin made of driftwood is the ultimate example of a home decor inspired by natural found objects.

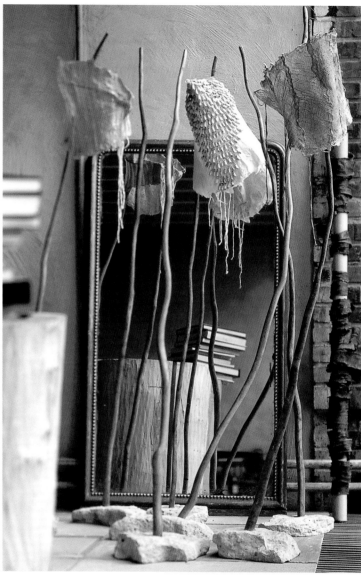

The abstract shapes of found objects lend themselves to sculptural display. Sections of weathered, vine-twisted tree branches are lined up like an installation of modern art in a home on the Indonesian island of Sumbawa.

(*above*) Weathered tree branches are incorporated into a formal sculptural group in this Flemish home, mounted on slabs of drilled stone and capped with handmade paper objects that resemble skins. A stack of books on an unfinished stump, reflected in the mirror, forms another part of the intensely organic assemblage.

(*opposite*) Dried, twisted rainforest vines – now an expensive decorative accessory in fashionable city florists – line the walls of an artist's studio in their native Indonesia.

(*opposite*) A row of elbow-shaped branches stacked behind an outdoor pipe: a perfect composition of breathtaking simplicity and wit.

(*right*) Graceful, phallic lengths of driftwood collected by an artist in Kenya, in an assemblage that is more organic than suggestive.

(*below right*) The natural shapes of certain pieces of driftwood seem almost representational to an imaginative eye. Mounted as sculptures, these pieces have a grotesque and ghostly aspect, like the 'angel' and 'horse's head' displayed outside the beach house of a Corsican artist.

It needs an unusually inventive mind to turn bleached pieces of wood into a majestic throne (*left*) or a rustic candelabra (*opposite*). Both examples come from Corsica. Their unfinished, prehistoric-looking shapes bring a note of primitive wildness to otherwise conventional interiors.

Rough-hewn sections of tree trunk serve as evocative chairs and display pedestals in this Belgian fashion designers' studio. A chandelier made from the roots of the same tree playfully inverts the expected order of things, creating the illusion that the roots are growing through the ceiling, feeding on the light and conversation rising from the room.

The heavily grained and crudely polished wood used for the slab table and chair brings a sophisticated naturalism to this home in Sumbawa, Indonesia, where traditional dug-out canoes, mounted on end, stand like monumental modern sculptures.

(*opposite*) Pebbles, glass and shells may be picked up on any beach and no two pieces are exactly alike. These tiny treasures from the sea offer endless opportunities for pattern-making, which can be intentionally representational or abstract and totally instinctive.

(*right*) Black beach pebbles on a table in a French home arranged in the shape of a face. The flickering candles, strange clay pipes and dark colours add a suggestion of black magic that keeps the arrangement from appearing completely light-hearted and trite.

Shells shine like jewels when they are first collected on a beach, but it is a considerable challenge to sustain the thrill of discovery when shells are displayed in the home, dried and no longer glistening in the sun. One solution is to show them in containers that are themselves visually interesting. Small shells cached inside larger shells suggest a natural treasure trove; a discovery of pearls inside an oyster. A handful of small shells from Kiwayu Island off the coast of Kenya is displayed in a clam shell (*left*). A collection of shells and bones gathered on the island of Sumbawa, east of Bali, includes the sea-washed backbone of a turtle displayed on the floor in a large shallow bowl (*opposite*).

Little Kenyan shells are casually arranged on shelves suspended from sisal ropes used on local boats. The display adds a fitting nautical context to the collection.

This six-sided cabinet in a house in Mexico is as eye-catching and unusual as the shells it contains. The drawers – each of which holds a perfect specimen of a different type of shell – invite the visitor to experience the thrill of discovery as each item is revealed in turn.

A collection of coral in a house in Bora Bora is displayed on unusual sculpted plaster shelves that themselves resemble a coral reef. The under-the-sea decorative effect is magical.

(*overleaf*) The old 'cabinets of curiosities' included all the things shown here – shells, minerals and stuffed birds – the only criterion being that they should all be visually interesting.

Cabinets of curiosities keep a collection of natural objects contained and protected from light and dust, while evoking the glamour of the gentleman–naturalists of old. The nets leaning against this cabinet filled with stuffed birds and eggs conjure up images of Victorian butterfly collectors.

The moths, insects and foreign curios neatly displayed in this antique museum case in a Paris home recall the great collections in stately homes of the Englightenment.

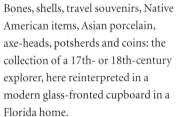

Bones, shells, travel souvenirs, Native American items, Asian porcelain, axe-heads, potsherds and coins: the collection of a 17th- or 18th-century explorer, here reinterpreted in a modern glass-fronted cupboard in a Florida home.

In another Florida home, feathers in a small glass case suggest a fantastic and slightly surreal museum display. The glass keeps the feathers from getting dusty or being blown away by drafts.

A handful of pebbles, a rustic cross, a model of a ship and a small gargoyle are curiously juxtaposed with everyday provisions on kitchen shelves.

(*above, opposite and overleaf*) Assemblages of bones, seed pods and old pictures in and around the home of artist and photographer Peter Beard in the Ngong Hills in Kenya.

Beard builds collections of found objects and photographs them, creating haunting artworks that comment on the rapid changes in modern Kenyan society threatening the local landscapes and traditional ways of life.

Found natural objects and photographs are an especially powerful combination in a decorative composition. This extraordinary creation, another of Beard's assemblages in the making, evokes the end of the culture of big-game hunting with fallen leaves on a faded photograph of the traditional quarry. The beads, stones, seeds and skulls surrounding the photograph suggest the centrality of the now-endangered big game to the entire culture and local ecosystem.

(*left*) Instead of pairing natural and found objects with photographs, this assemblage in a house in western France uses school yearbooks, art books and drawings for an equally evocative effect.

(*opposite*) This house on the Île de Ré belongs to a distinguished French designer, who has created a dramatic sculptural display from a whale vertebra and a single smooth stone.

(*overleaf*) A similar composition on the table in this Mexican house, where a single polished stone is displayed beside the rostra (bony toothed snout) of a sawfish. The bone is actually an antique; sawfish are now a critically endangered species.

(*above and opposite*) An artist's house on the Île de Ré is decorated with numerous installations mixing drawings, paintings and pictures with objects found on the beach: wave-tossed pebbles, metal sea-wrack (including fishing weights, rusted spikes and a section of a broken propeller) and painted and mounted fragments of driftwood.

Even though no two pieces are the same, the common source of their found materials – the sea – gives the installations visual coherence throughout the decor of the house.

(*above*) A playful display of driftwood in a house in Bolinas, California, presents one fragment of wood as a face and others as pieces of fine art enclosed by frames.

(*opposite*) If diamonds and pearls are jewels, why not driftwood and seed pods? Jewelry made from natural objects strung on to hemp cord and raffia hang from the wall of this French house like pieces in a sculptural installation, a device which could be copied by any discerning collector.

A few large rustic objects, prominently displayed, create a dramatic effect in a monochrome interior. Baskets and wooden bowls bring texture and warmth to the stripped floors and bare white walls of this redecorated Victorian townhouse in London, hinting at the elaborate fittings of wood and stone concealed by the paint.

Equally monochrome but warmer in
colour is this Provençal bedroom,
where willow baskets, exposed
beams, and rustic jewelry displayed
on a simple ladder give the feel of an
old-fashioned loggia in the American
Southwest.

Exposed beams and a massive plinth
constructed from a rough tree trunk
dominate the eclectic modern decor
of a room in Sumbawa, Indonesia.
Samples of Japanese fabric hang
from the wall like modern artworks.

(*above and opposite*) These rooms in a Mexican home have been decorated entirely from the owner's collection of natural objects and primitive artefacts from all over the world. They include a piece of snakeskin, a long seed pod from Madagascar, animal bones and a boomerang. Spotlights and a large gourd hang from rough timber beams. The floors are made of a heavily textured and banded local stone, which amplifies the naturalistic decorative theme and unifies the rustic collections arranged throughout the house.

CHAPTER 7

KITCHENALIA

Pre-plastic-era culinary paraphernalia
and its decorative possibilities

Culinary equipment might not be expected to have
decorative potential outside the kitchen, but plates,
bowls, tinware and old-fashioned utensils can look
even more interesting when displayed as artefacts of
an industrial age. Displayed in unexpected contexts
that emphasize the beauty of their design over their
practical functions, the forms of kitchen items seem
more pleasing, their patterns more artistic, their
textures more sensual. If whisks in the lounge don't
fit its decor, the kitchen itself can be made into a
gallery for display, even of practical items in
constant use. Shelves near the food preparation
areas can be set aside for especially beautiful items,
which should be carefully arranged, even if they are
continually removed and replaced during cooking.
The unusual shapes and cheerful colours of
kitchenalia will delight the eyes during the most
routine household chores.

This is not a kitchen, but its genesis – a discount store in New York
offering everything that the cook and the homemaker needs. The
stacks of dishes and containers hold countless decorative treasures.

(*left*) A kitchen imposes its own discipline on the decorator. One of its requirements is that everything – food, tools, dishes – must be easily accessible. Open shelves are essential in well-designed displays of kitchenalia. The upper two examples emphasize the utilitarian aspects of the displays, whereas the two lower examples are more self-consciously artistic, making dramatic use of a single strong colour in the walls and open shelves, which are decorated with serving dishes in the same shades.

(*opposite*) Open shelves displaying a collection of teapots and bowls create a semi-transparent partition between the dining room and the living room in the white, airy interior of a home on the Île de Ré.

A mixed collection of cooking implements lined up on a single long shelf suggests the practicality of a farmhouse kitchen, while adding a interesting horizontal element to the composition of a room. This traditional display of kitchen equipment comes from a house in Provence that is now a museum.

The same approach is used to display
a collection of antique American
pottery in a modern kitchen in
Milan. Although the shelving is
actually divided into three sections,
the consistent colour, shape and
texture of the sponge-ware jugs
lined up on the top shelves creates
the illusion of an unbroken
horizontal plane.

The kitchen is usually a part of the house that the owner arranges primarily to please him- or herself, rather than to impress guests. In breakfasting kitchens, however, one or two elements of formal display are often present for the benefit of guests. An Irish kitchen includes a collection of 'Brown Betty' teapots, proudly displayed on shelves over the refrigerator (*left*). An impressive, carefully composed display of white crockery makes a dramatic statement in an all-white kitchen in San Francisco, while the black occasional lamp and the mirrors hanging over the sink encourage the atmosphere of the living room to continue into the kitchen (*below left*).

(*right*) Gleaming pans and fresh fruit and herbs brighten a cheerful and unassuming kitchen in Ibiza.

(*below right*) In this Provençal kitchen, variations in texture: tarnished silver, galvanized steel, antique glass and pierced and fluted crockery break up the all-white colour scheme. The twisted willow branches framing the shelves are an unusual rustic decorative element, which also draws attention to the texture of the wooden cabinets. The careful attention to composition and colour suggests that this kitchen is meant to be seen as well as used.

Collections of ornamental crockery
are a class of kitchenalia routinely
displayed outside the kitchen. A
traditional wooden dresser is still
one of the most effective ways to
show off a set of treasured cups and
plates in a sitting room or dining
room, as in this display of Irish
sponge-ware in a Welsh home.

Cupboard doors faced with glass or wire netting allow a larger and more diverse collection of crockery to be displayed *en masse*. The different shapes, patterns and sizes of crockery stored in this cupboard in a Paris home resemble the chaotic jumble of a flea-market stall, but the cupboard lends coherence to the collection.

Kitchen compositions in France (*top left and right*), Corfu (*bottom left*) and Belgium (*bottom right*); four of the infinite number of ways in which pots and pans can be arranged on shelves, ranging from the traditional dresser and classic plate rack to a single plank on a bare wall.

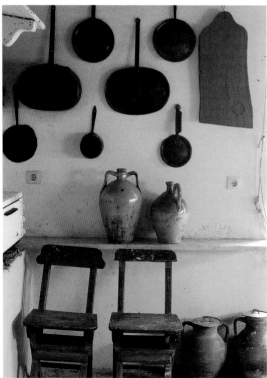

Shelf displays involving a clearly defined colour scheme are especially attractive, and can set the tone of an entire room. Blue-and-white assemblages from Wales (*top left*) and France (*top right*) have a cool, calming effect. The sunflower-yellow and turquoise elements in a pantry in Mexico (*bottom left*) and a dresser in Provence (*bottom right*) emphasize the warmth and liveliness of the kitchen space as well as the distinctive decorative styles of their respective countries.

Dense displays of china and glass contained in small cabinets give an explosive but controlled impression. A selection of drinking glasses in an old wooden cabinet in a kitchen in Budapest (*left*) reveals a careful balance of colour, texture and shape worthy of an installation in an art gallery. A more conventional display of modern kitchenware in a utilitarian steel shelving unit in a Paris home gives a no less carefully orchestrated expression of profusion and variety, with specialist equipment for cooking exotic foreign dishes displayed prominently on the open shelves (*opposite*).

(*opposite*) Glassware lends sparkle to dark rooms and minimalist decor, as in this simple display in a built-in cabinet of an house in Cooperstown, New York, which exemplifies the Puritan restraint of early 18th-century America.

(*right*) An array of figurative bottles, mostly for perfumes, makes an attractive display on a chest below a window, where it catches the light.

(*overleaf*) This traditional Swedish manor house kitchen at Tureholm was expressly designed to house decorative kitchenalia. With its elaborate blue and white paintwork – carried over in the furniture – and shelves up to the height of the ceiling, the whole room is transformed into an ornamental display cabinet for a stunning collection of antique Chinese and Delft porcelain.

(*pages 242–43*) A modern twist on the traditional idea of displaying decorative crockery outside the kitchen: a selection of intact and broken plates, cups, trivets and vases – probably collected from flea markets and recycling centres – are used as tiles in a giant wall mosaic.

(*left and below left*) Antique kitchen vessels made from half-glazed stoneware give a subtle two-toned and dual-textured effect when grouped together on a shelf or mantelpiece, as in these two houses in France.

Ingenious ways of storing dishes and utensils so that they are out of harm's way but still accessible: plates and mugs hanging from a specially built rack in a kitchen in Bohemia (*right*); wooden spoons and forks – some decorative, others in constant use – are slotted into grooves in a strip of wood (*below right*).

The repetition of a single type of kitchen item can give a spectacular decorative result. An incredible collection of antique mixing bowls dominates the dining room of a house in the Hamptons, Long Island, New York. The plain white shelves draw attention to the subtle variations in size and pattern between the bowls, hinting at the thousands of different recipes that might have been made in them. The upper shelves in this carefully structured display hold antique model boats and children's toys, while the shelves in the adjoining hallway are lined with colourful 1940s and 1950s Fiestaware. The furniture and floors are plain, encouraging the white shelves and their contents to stand out even more brightly.

(*opposite*) Modern city-dwellers, increasingly dependent on technology for every aspect of their daily lives, are experiencing a wave of nostalgia for a time before plastics. This Paris kitchen cultivates a deliberate rustic look, retaining unfinished surfaces and making extensive use of fixtures and utensils recycled from a bygone age. What at first glance appears to be the kitchen of a hastily outfitted squat is in fact an expensive apartment decorated with antiques.

(*right*)A different interpretation of the rustic look in another modern French kitchen. Nothing in this kitchen is plastic or electronic. Traditional earthenware jugs and glass bottles, a wooden chopping board and even an antique baker's scale adorn the plain wooden work surfaces, while woven baskets soften the glare of wire rolling racks. Lighting is simple and utilitarian, and also avoids using plastic, giving the modern fixtures a more timeless look. On the top shelf, a line of colourful pottery – a typical decorative display in old-fashioned country kitchens – adds a band of colour and pattern.

(*left*) Tin and copper moulds for chocolate, cake and gelatin have wonderful decorative potential due to their shine and availability in a variety of interesting shapes. A row of chocolate moulds adorns a wall in a home on the Île de Ré, their matching halves radiating symmetrically outward from a central light fixture that maximizes the shine of the tin at night.

(*opposite*) A beautiful, surreal assemblage of chocolate moulds in the shape of fish and other symbolically potent forms, elegantly arranged against the yellow walls of the kitchen in the same house, complementing the silver tube of the old-fashioned stove and a collection of antique metal tools.

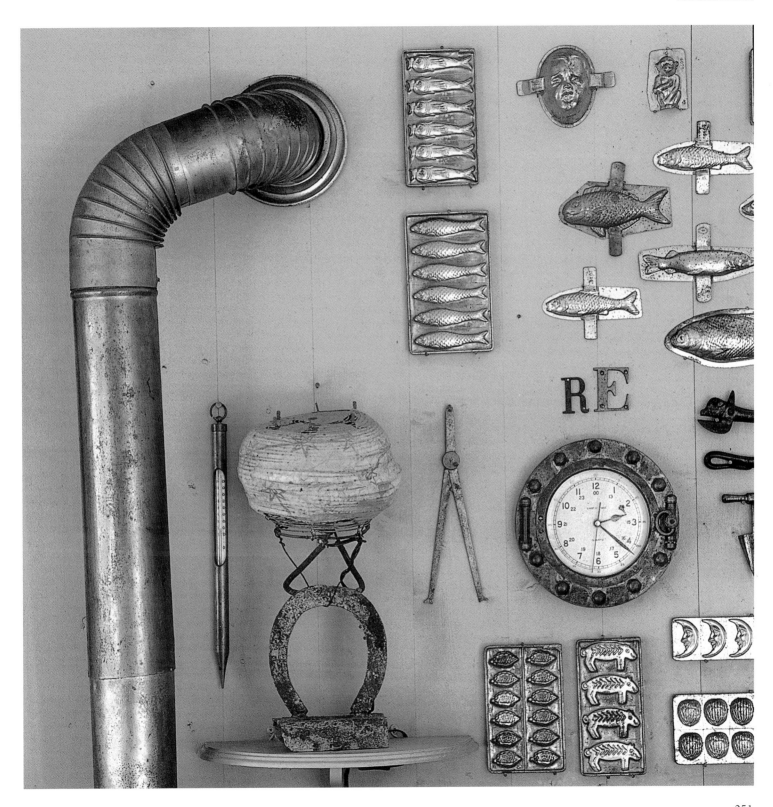

(*left*) Vintage kitchen appliances can be used as striking decorative focal pieces outside the kitchen. An all-in-one kitchen console from the 1930s, with inbuilt clock and plate warmer, grounds the retro-futuristic decorative theme of a pink and aqua Paris apartment.

(*opposite*) A restored street vendor's food cart makes a suprisingly sophisticated display piece, appropriately paired with old café chairs in a Provençal dining room.

ACKNOWLEDGMENTS

This book is dedicated to Robert Adkinson, who – until his retirement in 2008 – committed himself with tremendous enthusiasm and loyalty to the development and production of *The Way We Live* series of books.

Designed by Stafford Cliff
Index compiled by Pamela Ellis

First published in the United States of America in 2009 by
Rizzoli International Publications, Inc.
300 Park Avenue South
New York, NY 10010
www.rizzoliusa.com

Originally published in the United Kingdom in 2009 by
Thames & Hudson Ltd
181A High Holborn
London WC1V 7QX

The Way We Live: With the Things We Love
© 2009 Thames & Hudson Ltd, London

All photographs
© 2009 Estate of Gilles de Chabaneix

Design and layout
© 2009 Stafford Cliff

Text and captions
© 2009 Thames & Hudson Ltd, London

ISBN: 978-0-8478-3225-5

Library of Congress Control Number:
2008934691

2009 2010 2011 2012 / 10 9 8 7 6 5 4 3 2 1

Printed and bound in Singapore by CS Graphics

The photographs in *The Way We Live* series of books are the result of many years of travelling around the world to carry out commissions for various publications.
Very special thanks is due to Catherine de Chabaneix, for all her help during the production of this book, and for her ongoing commitment to Gilles' remarkable archive.
In addition, thanks to all the people who have helped to make the realization of this series possible, including Martine Albertin, Béatrice Amagat, Catherine Ardouin, Françoise Ayxandri, Marion Bayle, Jean-Pascal Billaud, Anna Bini, Marie-Claire Blanckaert, Barbara Bourgois, Marie-France Boyer, Marianne Chedid, Alexandra D'Arnoux, Jean Demachy, Emmanuel de Toma, Geneviève Dortignac, Jérôme Dumoulin, Marie-Claude Dumoulin, Lydia Fiasoli, Jean-Noel Forestier, Marie Kalt, Françoise Labro, Anne Lefèvre, Hélène Lafforgue, Catherine Laroche, Nathalie Leffol, Blandine Leroy, Marianne Lohse, Véronique Méry, Chris O'Byrne, Christine Puech, José Postic, Nello Renault, Daniel Rozensztroch, Elisabeth Selse, Suzanne Slesin, Caroline Tiné, Francine Vormèse, Claude Vuillermet, Suzanne Walker, Rosaria Zucconi and Martin Bouazis.

Our thanks also go to those who allowed Gilles access to their houses and apartments: Jean-Marie Amat, Mea Argentieri, Avril, Claire Basler, Bébèche, Luisa Becaria, Dominique Bernard, Dorothée Boissier, Carole Bracq, Susie and Mark Buell, Michel Camus, Laurence Clark, Anita Coppet and Jean-Jacques Driewir, David Cornell, Bertile Cornet, Jane Cumberbatch, Geneviève Cuvelier, Ricardo Dalasi, Anne and Pierre Damour, Catherine Dénoual, Dominique and Pierre Bénard Dépalle, Phillip Dixon, Ann Dong, Patrice Doppelt, Philippe Duboy, Christian Duc, Jan Duclos Maïm, Bernard Dufour, Explora Group, Flemish Primitives, Michèle Fouks, Pierre Fuger, Massimiliano Fuksas, Teresa Fung and Teresa Roviras, Henriette Gaillard, Jean and Isabelle Garçon, John MacGlenaghan, Fiora Gondolfi, Annick Goutal and Alain Meunier, Murielle Grateau, Michel and Christine Guérard, Yves and Michèle Halard, Hotel Le Sénéchal, Hotel Samod Haveli, Anthony Hudson, Ann Huybens, Patrick T'Hoft, Igor and Lili, Michèle Iodice, Paul Jacquette, Hellson, Jolie Kelter and Michael Malcé, Amr Khalil, Dominique Kieffer,

Kiwayu Safari Village, Lawrence and William Kriegel, Philippe Labro, Karl Lagerfeld, François Lafanour, Nad Laroche, Rudolph Thomas Leimbacher, Philippe Lévèque and Claude Terrijn, Marion Lesage, Lizard Island Hotel, Luna, Catherine Margaretis, Marongiu, Mathias, Valérie Mazerat and Bernard Ghèzy, Jean-Louis Mennesson, Ilaria Miani, Anna Moï, Leonardo Mondadori, Jacqueline Morabito, Christine Moussière, Paola Navone, Christine Nicaise, Christian Neirynck, Jean Oddes, Catherine Painvin, John Pawson, Christiane Perrochon, Phong Pfeufer, Françoise Pialoux les Terrasses, Alberto Pinto, Stéphane Plassier, Morgan Puett, Bob Ramirez, Riad Dar Amane, Riad Dar Kawa, Yagura Rié, Guillaume Saalburg, Holly Salomon, Jérôme-Abel Séguin, Jocelyne and Jean-Louis Sibuet, Siegrid and her cousins, Valérie Solvi, Tapropane Villa, Patis and Tito Tesoro, Richard Texier, Jérôme Tisné, Doug Tomkins, Anna and Patrice Touron, Christian Tortu, Armand Ventilo, Véronique Vial, Barbara de Vries, Thomas Wegner, Quentin Wilbaux, Catherine Willis.

Thanks are also due to the following magazines for allowing us to include photographs originally published by them: *Architectural Digest* (French Edition), *Atmosphère*, *Coté Sud*, *Elle*, *Elle à Table*, *Elle Décoration*, *Elle Décor Italie*, *Madame Figaro*, *Maison Française*, *Marie Claire*, *Marie Claire Idées*, *Marie Claire Maison*, *The World of Interiors*.

Page 88–9 The London Art Fair is the UK's largest and most established art fair, providing a unique opportunity to see and buy the best in modern British and contemporary art from the last 100 years, at prices from £50 to £500,000.
www.londonartfair.co.uk